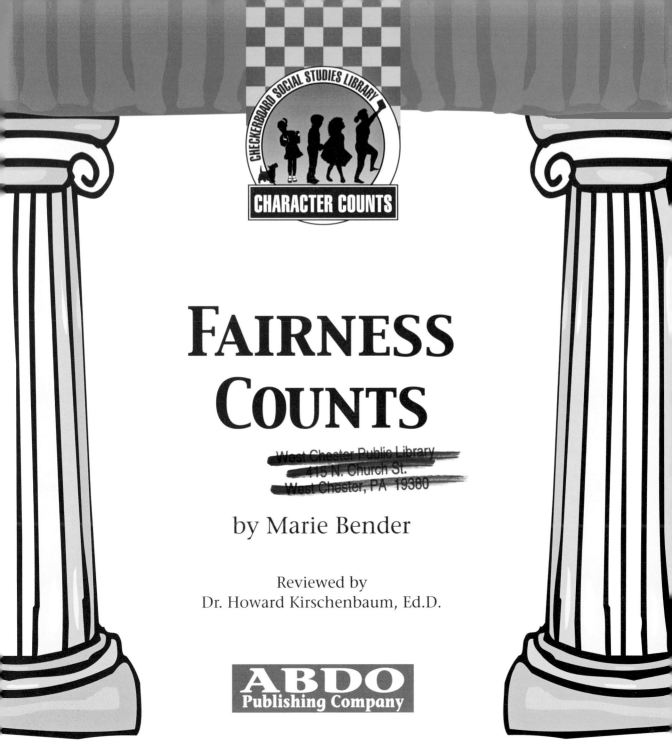

CHECKERBOARD SOCIAL STUDIES LIBRARY

CHARACTER COUNTS

FAIRNESS COUNTS

by Marie Bender

Reviewed by
Dr. Howard Kirschenbaum, Ed.D.

ABDO
Publishing Company

visit us at
www.abdopub.com

Published by ABDO Publishing Company, 4940 Viking Drive, Edina, Minnesota 55435. Copyright © 2003 by Abdo Consulting Group, Inc. International copyrights reserved in all countries. No part of this book may be reproduced in any form without written permission from the publisher.

Printed in the United States.

Photo credits: BananaStock Ltd., Brand X Pictures, Comstock, Corbis Images, Digital Vision, Eyewire Images, PhotoDisc, Skjold Photography, Stockbyte

Editors: Kate A. Conley, Stephanie Hedlund

Design and production: Mighty Media

Library of Congress Cataloging-in-Publication Data

Bender, Marie, 1968-
    Fairness counts / Marie Bender.
      p. cm. -- (Character counts)
    Summary: Defines fairness as a character trait and discusses how to show fairness at home, with friends, at school, in the community, and toward oneself.
    Includes index.
    ISBN 1-57765-870-1
    1. Fairness--Juvenile literature. [1. Fairness.] I. Title.

BJ1533.F2 B46 2002
179'.9--dc21

                                                    2002074500

Internationally known educator and author Howard Kirschenbaum has worked with schools, non-profit organizations, governmental agencies, and private businesses around the world to develop school/family/community relations and values education programs for more than 30 years. He has written more than 20 books about character education, including a high school curriculum. Dr. Kirschenbaum is currently the Frontier Professor of School, Family, and Community Relations at the University of Rochester and teaches classes in counseling and human development.

CONTENTS

Character Counts 4

What is Fairness? 8

Fairness and Family 12

Fairness and Friends 16

Fairness and School 20

Fairness and Community 23

Being Fair to Yourself 26

It's Not Fair! 28

Glossary 31

Web Sites 31

Index 32

CHARACTER COUNTS

The true test of character is not how much we know how to do, but how we behave when we don't know what to do.

—John Holt, author

Your character is the combination of **traits** that makes you an individual. It's not your physical traits, such as the color of your eyes or how tall you are. Rather, character is your thoughts, feelings, beliefs, and values.

Your character shows in the way you interact with your family, friends, teachers, and other community members. People who are well liked and successful are said to have a good character. Many traits build good character. Some of these traits include caring, fairness, honesty, good citizenship, responsibility, and respect.

Fairness Counts

Patricia's friend Martha came over to her apartment after school. They were playing checkers when Patricia's sister, Alison, came home. Alison said that she and her friend, Samantha, wanted to play checkers, too. Patricia said, "Too bad! Martha and I are playing, so you'll just have to do something else."

Alison said, "No! It's my game, too, and you've been using it for a while so it's my turn now!"

Patricia could see that it was going to turn into a big fight, so she thought of a way that they could all play. "Why don't we have a tournament?" she said. "Alison, you play the winner of the game Martha and I are playing now, and then Samantha will play the winner of your game, and so on. Each time someone loses, she goes to the end of the line. We'll see who can win the most games in a row."

Alison said, "Okay, that sounds like fun!"

Patricia made fairness count. ◾

WHAT IS FAIRNESS?

This country will not be a good place for any of us to live in unless we make it a good place for all of us to live in.

—Theodore Roosevelt, twenty-sixth president of the United States

Fairness is acting on the belief that everyone is equal and deserves the same opportunities. Fairness is treating others the way you want to be treated. When you are fair to others, they will likely be fair to you in return.

Being fair means wanting others to have the same chances, possessions, or **rights** that you have. Fairness does not mean that everything is always equal. Sometimes situations prevent you from having the same chances, possessions, or rights that others have. Being fair means accepting others who have something you don't.

Many values make up a fair person. Equality, **tolerance**, and acceptance are forms of fairness. There are many ways to **demonstrate** these values. You can show that

Think about it...

What can you do to show you are fair?

How do you feel when you have been treated unfairly?

What does that teach you about how to treat others?

8

The Golden Rule
Around the World

Hurt not others in ways that you yourself would find hurtful. —Buddha

So whatever you wish that men would do to you, do so to them; for this is the law and the prophets. —*The Gospel of Matthew*

Do not do to others what you do not want them to do to you. —Confucius

Do naught unto others which would cause you pain if done to you. —*The Mahabarata*

No one of you is a believer until he desires for his brother that which he desires for himself. —Muhammad

What is hateful to you, do not to your fellow man. —*The Talmud*

Regard your neighbor's gain as your own gain, and your neighbor's loss as your own loss. —Tai Shang Kan Ying P'ien

9

FAIRNESS

you are fair by sharing with others and taking turns. You can follow the rules at home, at school, and in your community. You can also accept others for who they are, not the way they look, talk, or dress.

Have you ever wondered what it would be like if no one was treated fairly? Without fairness, people would be selfish. People would lie, cheat, and steal because no one would care about the **rights** of others. No one would have friends because people would not trust each other. No one would have fun because everyone would cheat. No one would feel safe because people would not obey laws or follow rules. Without fairness, the world would be a dangerous, lonely place.

However, fairness does exist, and you can see it every day. You can see fairness when people include others in their activities, take turns, or share. You can see fairness when people treat others equally. You can also see it when people work to make sure everyone has adequate food, shelter, education, and health care. The great thing about fairness is that if you treat others fairly, they will be more likely to treat you fairly. And knowing that you are a fair person makes you feel good about yourself.

Think about it...

What do you think might happen if fairness didn't exist?

What are some examples that show fairness does exist?

FAIRNESS AND FAMILY

It is not fair to ask of others what you are not willing to do yourself.

—Eleanor Roosevelt, first lady and American stateswoman

Fairness is usually learned from your family. Your family can do many things to show that being fair is important. For instance, you can share and take turns to show your family you are willing to **compromise**.

Your parents have rules for you and your **siblings**. These rules are made to keep everyone safe and establish responsibility. You can follow the rules to show you are a fair person. Some rules may seem unfair, such as your older brother having a later bedtime than you. But fair doesn't always mean things are exactly the same. When you are older, you will get to stay up later, too. That is fair.

FAIRNESS

Fairness in your family also means not acting **jealously** when it is someone else's turn to get something special. When your sister receives presents on her birthday, or your brother gets a reward for doing well on his history test, you can be fair by not getting jealous. Parents and other relatives try to treat family members equally for special events, holidays, and accomplishments. It is fair to share in the good will toward each person because when it is your turn, you want others to feel happy for you.

FAIRNESS

Many families have to share things, such as a television or computer. So it is important to **compromise** so everyone gets a turn. If you and your sister both need to use the computer to do homework, it is fair to take turns so that you can both get your work done. Family members also have to share the house or apartment where they live. You can be fair by cleaning up after yourself and doing your share of chores.

Think about it...

What are some of the rules in your family?

Do you think they are fair?

What has your family taught you about fairness?

FAIRNESS AND FRIENDS

Play fair. Don't hit people. Say you're sorry when you hurt somebody.
—Robert Fulghum, author

Your friends are very important and treating them fairly strengthens your relationships with them. If you were to treat others unfairly, you would not have any friends. People dislike spending time with those who are unfair, selfish, or dishonest. Being fair makes it easy for your friends to trust and like you. And that makes you feel good about yourself.

You can be fair by taking turns when you are with your friends. If you want to spend Saturday afternoon riding bikes, but your friend wants to play board games, you can decide to play games for a while, and then ride bikes for a while. That is a fair **compromise** because you will both get to do what you want. You will not waste time arguing about what to do.

Being fair with your friends means sharing with them. Your friends are responsible for taking care of what you lend them. You can share to show others you are not a selfish person.

Sometimes you may get something new that your friends wish they had. Friends try not to be **jealous** of each other in these situations. When you get something that others want, you want them to be happy for you, not jealous. Likewise, your friends may get things that you want. It may be hard for you not to get jealous. But it is not your friend's fault you don't have what they do. So it is not fair to blame your friend for your own disappointment. It may not seem fair when others get things you don't, but feeling jealous can hurt your friendships.

Being fair with your friends means being honest. This means that you tell the truth, follow the rules, and do not cheat. It feels good to win a game. But if you win by cheating, it's less rewarding because you know that you don't really deserve it. You know it is unfair. The fair thing to do is to play honestly, and when your friend wins, be happy for him or her. The point of games is to have fun and share time together, even if you lose.

FAIRNESS

How do you feel when one of your friends treats you unfairly?

How can you let your friend know that you think he or she was unfair?

FAIRNESS AND SCHOOL

Here's my Golden Rule for a tarnished age: Be fair with others, but keep after them until they're fair with you.

—*Alan Alda, actor*

Fairness at school means following the rules. Rules make your school a safe place so every student has a chance to learn. When you disobey the rules, you are acting unfairly. Disobeying the rules means you think you do not have to be treated the same way as others. You are taking unfair advantage of others when you do not follow the rules.

FAIRNESS

Acting fairly at school means you respect the **rights** of your classmates. If you disrupt class, others have a hard time paying attention, and that isn't fair. You can be fair by participating in class discussions and listening to what your teachers and classmates say. You can also be fair by waiting for your

turn to speak and not interrupting others. It's not fair to copy test answers from the classmate sitting next to you or to get someone else to do your homework. That is cheating. Cheating is unfair and dishonest.

Fairness also means being friendly to your classmates and not teasing children who seem different than you. When you play a game at recess, it is fair to include everyone who wants to play. And if everyone cannot play at the same time, it's fair to take turns.

Working on group projects in school is a way to meet classmates you might not usually get to know. Getting to know students other than your close friends is fair, respectful, and kind. It doesn't mean you have to be best friends with them, but it will give you a chance to get to know other people. Even if you don't end up as friends, you can be fair to them by respecting their **right** to be who they are.

Think about it...

What are some unfair things that happen at school?

Is everyone treated equally at your school?

FAIRNESS AND COMMUNITY

These men ask for just the same thing—fairness, and fairness only. This, so far as in my power, they, and all others, shall have.

—Abraham Lincoln, sixteenth president of the United States

Being fair in your community means following laws and treating people with respect. Laws are for everyone to follow so that your community will be a safe and peaceful place to live. When people break laws, it is unfair to those who follow them.

You can show fairness in your community in several ways. You can give pedestrians the right of way when you are riding your bike or skateboard on the sidewalk. You can walk in crosswalks at intersections when the traffic lights say "walk." Walking when "don't walk" lights are flashing is dangerous and can cause an accident. You can also be fair by walking your dog on a leash. The leash will keep your dog from running away and scaring other people.

Respecting differences in your community is a way to show that you are fair. Many people in your community are different from you. Some people are older, from a different country, speak a different language, look or dress differently, or have different beliefs. It is fair to treat everyone the same way you want to be treated. It is also fair to do what you can to improve your community, so everyone has equal opportunities.

It is also fair to respect other people's property. Everyone has the **right** to keep his or her yard looking the way he or she wants. It wouldn't be fair to trample someone's garden when you are playing with your friends or to throw litter in someone's yard.

FAIRNESS

The same **rights** apply to public areas, such as parks and community centers. Tax money and **donations** help your community create places like these for everyone. If you use your local park or community center, it is fair to help take care of it so it stays nice. Everyone has the right to live in a peaceful neighborhood. So it's not fair to play loud music late at night or run wildly down apartment building hallways.

What are some ways you can show you are fair in your community?

Can you think of some examples of things in your community that do not seem fair?

BEING FAIR TO YOURSELF

I know, up on top you are seeing great sights, but down at the bottom we, too, should have some rights.

—Dr. Seuss, author

It is important to remember to be fair to yourself. It is easy to think about others before you think about yourself. When you think about treating others like you want to be treated, you know that being fair and respectful are **traits** that you value. Being fair means being honest and **impartial** and not selfish or **prejudiced**. When you are a fair person, others count on you to be trustworthy. If you say you are going to do something, do it. It builds your self-esteem and self-confidence to face situations that require you to act fairly. These situations also build good character and make you a better person.

FAIRNESS

It's Not Fair!

Men, their rights and nothing more, women their rights and nothing less. —*Susan B. Anthony, women's rights activist*

How many times have you said or heard another person say, "It's not fair!"? It seems this phrase is used frequently. But you must remember that what is fair in one situation may not be fair in another. For example, it may not seem fair that younger children have earlier **curfews** than older children do. But it is fair for children who are the same age to have the same curfew. It may not seem fair that high school students usually have more homework than elementary school students. But it is fair for everyone in the same grade to have the same amount of homework.

Determining fairness and how it applies to different situations can be difficult. As you get older, you will learn what it means for you to be a fair person and how it affects your life. Being fair shows you have the ability to be a good leader at home, at school, and in your community.

Glossary

compromise - settling an argument by having each side give up part of its demand.

curfew - a rule that requires a person to be home by a certain time.

demonstrate - to make a show of; express openly.

donation - a gift.

impartial - not favoring one over another.

jealous - envious of another person's possessions or accomplishments.

prejudice - an often negative opinion formed without knowing all the facts.

right - a legal or moral claim to something.

sibling - a brother or sister.

tolerance - a willingness to accept other people's behaviors or customs.

trait - a quality that distinguishes one person or group from another.

Web Sites

Would you like to learn more about character? Please visit www.abdopub.com to find up-to-date Web site links about caring, fairness, honesty, good citizenship, responsibility, and respect. These links are routinely monitored and updated to provide the most current information available.

INDEX

C

caring 4
character traits 4, 26
classmates 21, 22
community 4, 11, 23, 24, 25, 28

E

equality 8, 11, 12, 20, 21, 24

F

fairness 4, 8, 11, 12, 13, 15, 16, 19, 20, 21, 22, 23, 24, 25, 26, 28
family 4, 12, 13, 15
feelings 4, 19
friends 4, 11, 16, 19, 22

G

good citizenship 4

H

honesty 4, 16, 19, 21, 26

L

laws 11, 23

N

neighborhood 25

P

parents 12, 13

R

respect 4, 23, 24, 26
responsibility 4, 12
rights 8, 11, 21, 22, 24, 25
rules 11, 12, 19, 20

S

school 11, 20, 21, 22, 28
sharing 11, 12, 13, 15, 16, 19
siblings 12, 13, 15

T

teachers 4, 21

V

values 4, 8

For the Character Counts series, ABDO Publishing Company researched leading character education resources and references in an effort to present accurate information about developing good character and why doing so is important. While the title of the series is Character Counts, these books do not represent the Character Counts organization or its mission. ABDO Publishing Company recognizes and thanks the numerous organizations that provide information and support for building good character in school, at home, and in the community.